Monday	GP
Tuesday	Swimming
Wednesday	
Thursday	Art class
Friday	
Saturday	Shopping
Sunday	

SPACE POPS

milk

2

3

Monday	GP
Tuesday	Swimming
Wednesday	
Thursday	Art class
Friday	
Saturday	Shopping
Sunday	

SPACE POPS

4

Monday	GP
Tuesday	Swimming
Wednesday	
Thursday	Art class
Friday	
Saturday	Shopping
Sunday	

SPACE POPS

milk

Monday	GP
Tuesday	Swimming
Wednesday	
Thursday	Art class
Friday	
Saturday	Shopping
Sunday	

SPACE
POPS

milk

6